Table of Contents

Y0-CZM-713

Twinkle, Twinkle, Little Star

Twin - kle, twin - kle, li - ttle star,

How I won - der what you are.

Up a - bove the world so high,

Like a dia - mond in the sky.

Twin - kle, twin - kle, li - ttle star,

How I won - der what you are.

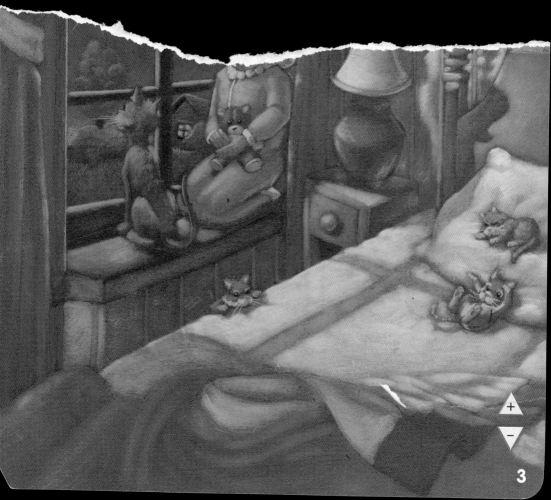

3

Hickory, Dickory, Dock

Hick - o - ry, dick - o - ry, dock,

The mouse ran up the clock.

The clock struck one; The mouse ran down,

Hick - o - ry, dick - o - ry, dock.

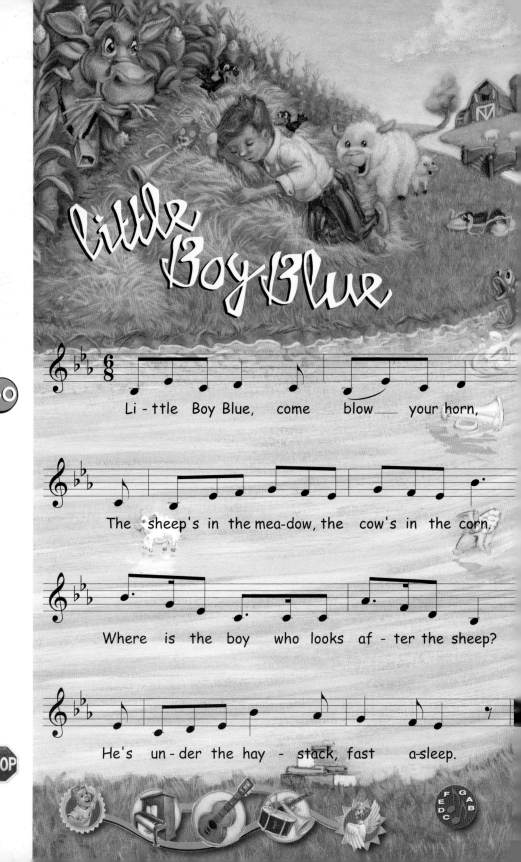

Little Boy Blue

Li - ttle Boy Blue, come blow your horn,

The sheep's in the mea-dow, the cow's in the corn.

Where is the boy who looks af - ter the sheep?

He's un - der the hay - stack, fast a-sleep.

Sing a Song of Sixpence

Sing a song of six - pence, A po-cket full of rye;

Four and twen-ty black - birds Baked in a pie.

When the pie was o - pened, The birds be-gan to sing.

Wa-sn't that a dain-ty dish To set be-fore the king?

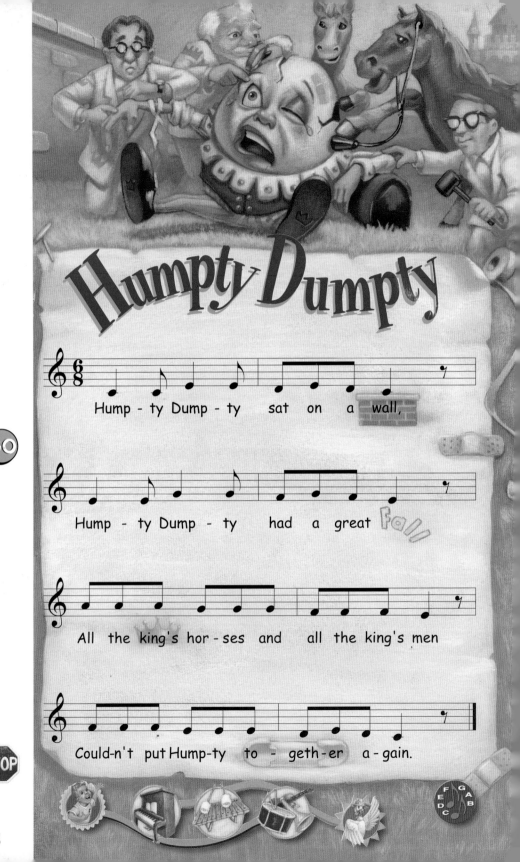

Little Jack Horner

Li - ttle Jack Hor - ner sat in a cor - ner,

Ea - ting his mince - meat pie.

He stuck in his thumb And pulled out a plum,

And said, "What a good boy am I!"

Itsy, Bitsy Spider

The It - sy Bit - sy spi - der

Climbed up the wa - ter - spout.

Down came the rain

And washed the spi - der out.

GO

STOP

10

Out came the sun

And dried up all the rain;

And the It - sy Bit - sy spi der

Climbed up the spout a - gain.

It's Raining, It's Pouring

It's rain - ing, it's pour - - ing;

The old man is snor - ing.

Bumped his head And he went to bed

And he could-n't get up in the morn - ing.

Jack & Jill

Jack and Jill went up the hill,

To fetch a pail of wa - ter;

Jack fell down and broke his crown,

And Jill came tum - bling af - ter.

Little Miss Muffet

Li - ttle Miss Mu - ffet sat on a tu - ffet,

Ea - ting her curds and whey;

A - long came a spi - der Who sat down be - side her

And frigh - tened Miss Mu - ffet a - way.

GO

STOP

Where has my little dog gone?

Oh, where, oh, where has my li-ttle dog gone?

Oh, where, oh, where can he be?

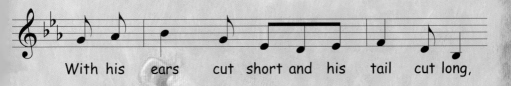

With his ears cut short and his tail cut long,

Oh, where, oh, where can he be?

Hey, di-ddle, di-ddle, The cat and the fid-dle,

The cow jumped o-ver the moon.

The lit-tle dog laughed to see such sport,

And the dish ran a-way with the spoon.

Piano Play

Climbing
Start on Spider's piano key!

Climb – ing

Climb – ing

Up   we   go!

Going Low
Start on Honeybee's piano key!

Higher and Lowe

Step – ping

down – ward

We   go   low.

GO

STOP

C D E F G A B C D E

18

Mary Had A Little Lamb

Ma - ry   had   a   li - ttle   lamb,

li - ttle   lamb,   li - ttle   lamb.

Ma - ry   had   a   li - ttle   lamb,

whose   fleece   was   white   as   snow.

F G A B C D E F G A